Praise for

"A truly empowering read for anyone who is a patient, survivor, caregiver or clinician. With various relatable anecdotes and opportunities for self-reflection, I have no doubt that it will make the journey easier and offer strength in the darkest of times. As a medical professional it is a book I will strongly recommend to my patients, with any significant or chronic condition. It is also of huge benefit to my medical colleagues, to really submerge ourselves in the journey through the eyes of the patient themselves, inspiring us to deliver more holistic care."

Dr Nikhil Chatrath
Royal Brompton Hospital, London, UK

"A beautiful combination of spiritual and emotional support with pragmatic words for those entering the unexpected cancer journey. I really loved the scripting – especially around asking for help and around self-worth. I am excited to share this with patients."

Dr Adrienne Allen MD
Mass General Brigham, Boston, USA, and Physician Founder of Gesundheit Partners Digital Health Platform

"Rashmin's beautifully crafted words provide just what is needed when facing a cancer diagnosis. Packed with practical advice, gentle compassion, humble wisdom and radiant hope, this book will be a valued companion on a difficult journey."

Dr Laura Jarvie
GP partner and clinical director, Nelson Medical Practice, London, UK

"An exquisite and compelling account of her cancer diagnosis."
Ira Mathur
Journalist, writer and author of Love the Dark Days, *winner of the 2023 OCM Bocas Prize for Non-Fiction*

"I have been a cancer nurse for thirty years and found so much of what Rashmin writes about echoed by many other patients and families trying to understand what a diagnosis of cancer might mean for them. A cancer diagnosis arrives like a hurricane without warning and changes the world for the person and their loved ones. This beautifully written book of gentle wisdom and moments of pause will help the reader to find stillness and a chance to process. The book is more than this though, there are useful practical tips that only come from someone that has lived through this experience. I hear from people with cancer how difficult it is to tell others about being diagnosed and Rashmin gives actual words that can be used to start these difficult but important conversations.
Rashmin's book gives such invaluable insight into the experience of someone diagnosed with a rare cancer like sarcoma as well as someone from the Sikh and Indian communities."
Sam Hackett
Sarcoma Specialist Nurse, Sarcoma UK

This edition published in the UK in 2024

Copyright © Rashmin Sagoo 2024

The right of Rashmin Sagoo to be identified as the author of this work has been asserted under the Copyright, Designs and Patents Act 1988.

All rights reserved. No part of this publication may be reproduced, stored in a retrieval system, or transmitted in any form or by any means, electronic, mechanical, photocopying, recording or otherwise, without the prior written consent of the publishers.

No generative AI was used in creating this book.

Text and cover design by Caroline Goldsmith.
Cover image by Rashmin Sagoo

Also available as an ebook edition

Falling Leaves and Flying Butterflies

A cancer companion

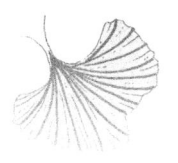

Rashmin Sagoo

For my Tree.

For my ancestral roots, that kept me grounded. For my son who kept me standing upright. And for all the different branches of my life that loved, sheltered, nourished, broke and regrew with me throughout the ferocious storm. Thank you for gently turning my face to the sun every morning.

Contents

Dear reader..11
How to use this book......................................13
Dear Nat..15
My story...17
Ki haal hai?..21
Telling People..22
"How can I help?"...29
What do you need right now?..........................31
Accepting help...34
Your Tree..37
Asking for help..39
Preparing for medical appointments..................42
Self-care...45
Grounding...48
Rest before you need to..................................56
Gratitude..60
Joy..64
Children...71
Hope..74
Light..76
Energy..79
"Feeling the feels"...81
Bravery..84
Creativity...87

Stillness and silence..................................90
Prayer...94
For friends and family............................98
Gift ideas..100
My Tree..103
Epilogue...105
Your notes..114

A note on the cover art........................124
Acknowledgements.............................125
Useful resources and organisations..........127
About the Author.................................128

Dear reader

If I could just sit with you,
Hold your hand,
And turn our faces to the sun,
I would.

But here is the next best thing,
A collection of poetry, prompts and
wisdom that others shared with me,
Which I now pass to you.

In the hope that even
if things sometimes feel alone, hopeless,
and even broken beyond repair
You find light within
And know you are love
And loved.

How to use this book

My notebooks reveal hundreds of doodles, drawings, reminders, doctors' names, hospital appointments, questions to ask, and poems.

There's something cleansing about using your own hand to scribe on paper. It slows the world down, just for a moment.

Space has been provided in these pages including an extra section at the end for you to make your own notes and jot down your thoughts.

I originally started writing this book for my cousin, Nat, when she had a cancer scare.
Luckily, it was just a scare.
This letter, which I originally wrote for her, is now for you, dear reader.

Dear Nat,

No one knows what you're going through, except for you. Perhaps you're not even sure if you know yourself right now. My prayer-wish for you is that the little light within you helps you through these dark days. That this guide becomes your companion through the earliest of them. A companion that rests within you. To help fortify you for whatever is to come. Holding your hand as if I were right there beside you.

This book is yours. For a few minutes to pause, reflect, exhale, and allow in a little ease. Scribble, doodle, bend its spine. Keep it somewhere safe in the sanctuary of your home or throw it on the floor in rage. Let it soak up your tears. Take it with you wherever you go, or return to it now and then. Scribe amidst its pages your innermost thoughts and all your heart's desires. The things you're too scared to even whisper out loud. Flick through for notes that chime. Keep it for yourself. Or share it with loved ones to offer them a glimpse into your new world, and perhaps help you navigate it. Use it to take note of the fast and furious medical process – the name of yet another doctor or nurse you saw, or the questions you want to ask next time. Fall apart, into the deepest parts of you. And then steady yourself for what is to come. Take whatever you need and leave the rest. This is your own companion, guided by your hand and heart, with a little help from mine.

With love, light and grace
Rashmin x

My story

At the top of a small hill, in a leafy London suburb is the quiet station of South Merton. From the entrance, you can see the train tracks stretch before you and disappear into the horizon until they meet the sky. Birds dance between overgrown shrubs, welcoming each day with joy. Single-pointed focus on survival they eat, sleep, chirp and repeat. They reminded me every day to look up to the sun, and allow the white noise of the busy London Road to wash over me. This is the place where I would start each day as I journeyed to the Royal Marsden Hospital, a beacon of expertise and hope, for my cancer treatment.

Every day I would go there and back – for routine appointments, check-ups and almost two months of post-surgery radiotherapy. I did this until I was too weary and kindly family, neighbours and occasionally taxi drivers would chauffeur me, comforting me amid waves of nausea from the treatment.

I still love that station. Standing at the top of that hill makes my heart soar. It's a reminder that each day is a fresh start, to try again and put yesterday to rest. The train leaves, whether we get on or not. Simply by deciding to step on to the train, even for the bumpiest of rides could feel like the biggest leap.

Taking life one day at a time, sometimes just one step at a time, reminded me to slow down and that whatever I was feeling in that moment was perfectly OK. It might be dread of what the latest CT scan or ultrasound would reveal. Or happiness that the nausea had passed and that I could stand up straight that day. It might be anger that, in the early days, I was being asked by loved ones to keep my illness secret. Frustration that I didn't feel as self-sufficient as I usually do, or annoyance at myself for snapping at my family that morning. Later, wonderment of whether the post-surgery wounds would ever heal. Bereavement for the loss of parts of me, then appreciation that my femininity and womanhood is so much more. And deep gratitude for being alive. All those thoughts and feelings tumbled around in me, often within milliseconds of each other, just waiting for the train. It was exhausting.

I once confided in my neighbour, Julia – a wonderfully strong, thoughtful and compassionate woman a few decades my senior and a former psychologist and therapist – that I was sad about lashing out at my family without meaning to. She explained how she would tell her children that thoughts and feelings are "just weather". You try to notice them and let them pass, knowing that the next moment could be sunnier, or stormier. A grey cloud might block the sunlight for what might seem like an eternity. But it would pass. It might be raining now, but a rainbow could emerge. So, I (very slowly) learnt that like the weather, I had no choice but to accept these emotions and thoughts, sit with them and let them pass.

Telling family and friends about my cancer and dealing with their reactions was one of the hardest things I had to face. Many reached out offering help, support and, of course, wanting news on my treatment and health. I created a little WhatsApp group which I called my 'Tree' to manage the communication flow. I tried to keep my posts authentic but positive, knowing what I put out there I would receive. What flowed back was a wave of love. In the form of poems, wisdom, grace, guidance, prayers, food parcels, home-cooked freezer food, flowers, cards, recommendations for books, music, promises of outings, art, voice messages and – knowing my love for them - photos of trees from around the world. Honestly, it was overwhelming. And I realised that I was, in fact, supported by something like a tree, with roots deep in love and branches spreading around the world.

At times I did not know *how* to receive that abundance of love. I did not think myself worthy. It took time to love myself enough to accept the love of others who would help both me and my family, who were also suffering. By opening myself, I was enabling others to reach capacities of love that even they were unaware of. It was a big lesson for me in learning how to ask for help and how to receive it. It has helped me ever since.

This book is a result of those times. It is a collection of the wisdom and love poured into me by loved ones and from within myself. I can't tell you what happens next. But I do know this: there is more to you than you know. And now is the time to draw on it.

a small pause
amid the frenzy of appointments
and the chaos of the mind
to find your breath
and exhale
to let the tears flow and
your hand glide across the page
pour out your heart
what your lips dare not say
to prepare yourself
knowing that whatever comes
you are worthy
and deeply loved

Ki haal hai?

In Punjabi, *ki haal hai?* means *"how are you?"*. In the early days of a diagnosis, this three-word question can be the hardest one to respond to. But I only recently unlocked its real meaning. *Ki haal hai?* enquires, *"what is the state of your heart, in this breath?"*.

> *When someone asks you how you are, how do you respond? Is it an automatic "I'm fine"? How might you respond more authentically, at least to those closest to you?*
>
> *In this moment, right now, in this breath, what is the state of your heart?*

Telling people

Indian families are the most amazing and beautiful communities to belong to. We are a diaspora community spread far and wide. It reminds me of networks of trees all over the world, interconnected underground through a complicated maze of roots and shoots. Recognising when one is in trouble, they send out distress signals, drawing strength from and nourishing one another over great distances. (Trees honestly do this. It's remarkable.)

However, the very rhythm that can bring a whole community together in a heartbeat can sometimes also deplete a person and deprive them of their own voice. Happily things are changing, but there remains a whiff of taboo around cancer in many different communities, including my own. Telling people was one of the most difficult things I had to face.

Really, it comes down to fear. And fear breeds fear. Seeing someone's fragility can unleash one's own darkest fears. This can lead to unthinking and reactive comments and assumptions sometimes disguised as love. I tried to remember that most of the comments were well-intentioned. But some were thoughtless and too hard to bear. Some of the things I was told included: *It's private, why tell anyone?... People will judge you and your family- they will say there is cancer in the family...You must now change jobs as yours is too stressful...This will impact your brother's future marriage prospects...If you tell people, we will be inundated with calls from relatives around the world saying 'sorry that you're dying', no need to tell anyone about the surgery as it will be too overwhelming.*

There was a grain of truth in some of this. It wasn't how I wanted the world to be, but it is how it is.

Rooted in their previous experience of loved ones facing cancer, in the early days of my diagnosis, my parents' instinct was not to tell a soul about what was happening to me. At times it felt as though they were projecting their own fears onto me. Later, I learnt that they too were in pain, grieving with me, trying to protect me, and in need of space to process, and to conserve their energy. They were navigating something unimaginable, for which they would have traded places in a heartbeat.

My instinct was different. I wished to slowly and surely open my illness to a small trusted circle, which grew into a Tree of support not just for me, but my son, his father and for all of us. It was taking deep inner work to accept what was happening to me. So, the idea of not telling anyone felt alien and a waste of precious energy.

It also seemed like a missed opportunity to ask for help and lift the veil on some of our community's fears as an alternative to perpetuating the fear through silence. It caused rifts between my then husband and me; through a western eye, he couldn't understand why I was even having the discussion with my parents given it was my body.

I started small, limiting revealing my diagnosis only to those who needed to know. I used this time to begin wrapping my own head around it before confronting the sadness and desperation of those closest to me.

My parents were right that it didn't feel like the right time to tell the world. I told my brother, aunty, cousin, godmother, those who have loved me since forever and who would hold me upright no matter what came. Then my boss and my childminder as they needed to know, and later, friends and neighbours who I could depend on for practical and emotional support. And so on.

I realise this all sounds very methodical and organised. It wasn't. It was messy and organic. Seeing my resolve, my parents had come around and helped me to tell people, but arguments continued over who should be told. I learnt to trust my gut and I found a way that was right for me. Broadly, it came down to this – *does this feel like the right time and place to tell this person? Will they be able to help or hinder my healing?* All this influenced my decision to tell close friends and family about my own illness.

Years later, I lost two dear friends to cancer, both in their 40s: one just before and one during the pandemic. Tash's approach to her cancer diagnosis was one of brutal honesty. She blogged and messaged on the happy highs and brutal lows. My other friend chose not to tell a soul, other than her parents and best friend. Even at her funeral, only a few of us were allowed to know of her cancer. It felt strange, particularly when informing others of her passing but not being allowed to explain the cause of her young death. My own mum did not reveal her cancer even to her own sister. Only four of us knew initially. On my wedding day, much of the festivities were spent finding ways to prevent relatives hugging her too tightly when congratulating her so that she wouldn't end up back in hospital with burst stitches from the operation she'd just had. In her usual selfless way, she did not wish to take attention away from the planned festivities. But her silence then, which I later understood to also be shock and denial, confused and angered me, especially as I knew she (and we) all needed help to get through and that people would be there if we asked.

What I learnt from all this is that every person, and every cancer, is different. To whom, with whom, when and how you decide to tell your story is your call. There may be particular sensitivities to consider within your own family, community or workplace. Sometimes life will take the decision out of your hands and decide for you. As and when you are ready to tell others, the following may help:

Take your time to tell your story

This is a big personal decision based on your particular circumstances. Tell people only what you are happy to share, and when you are happy to share it. Once they know, they can't unknow. And like it or not, people can judge. There is value in first preserving a little time and space for you and those closest to you alone to process the news and work out what's best for your unique situation, before sharing the news with others. They too will need time to process, but let that not be your burden. Your specialist cancer nurse, counsellor or a support group may be able to provide some guidance or a listening ear before you are confronted with the questions, fears and even grief of others, no matter how well-meaning. Keep in mind that what you feel like sharing will also change over time and that's ok too.

Initially, focus on your close circle

I kept a small circle of trusted people who I knew had my back and my heart. They knew all that was happening. One or two of them would keep others informed periodically. Gradually, over time, my Tree expanded.

Keep it short, positive but truthful

This is not to say people can't or shouldn't face the truths of what you're dealing with. But in the early days and given the potential for negative comments that my parents had warned me of I tried to keep information short, positive but truthful to encourage supportive messages to come back and buoy me upwards. I used stock phrases to minimise too much communication and to protect my energy: *No news is good news, but we will update when we can./ Your prayers are all we need, I can feel them./ If I don't answer your messages, don't worry – I'm probably asleep/resting/ avoiding my phone to manage my fatigue/trying to be a "normal" mum. /I would love to have a chat or visitor. So if you're nearby let me know - but please don't be offended if I need to cancel at short notice./ I'm conserving my energy right now, so not up for visitors. But thank you for sending me your positive energy and prayers, I feel them.*

How do you want to tell your story?

"How can I help?"

Once loved ones had processed their shock, the overwhelming response was "How can I help? Is there anything you need?"

The easiest reaction was, "I'm fine, I have everything I need, thanks." But I wasn't fine. I *did* need help. *We* needed help, my family and I. I just wasn't used to asking for it. I already felt intensely guilty for uprooting my loved ones who were distraught with my diagnosis and selfish for overwhelming them with my needs, let alone burdening others. After a while, I realised when people offer help, they usually mean it. And they knew I would do the same if the roles were reversed.

Some people struggled with *how* to help. I found myself simultaneously between two contrasting cultures – a British one where people wanted to help but didn't wish to "impose" or "intrude" so sometimes held back; and an Indian one where loved ones would swoop in and help before I even knew what I needed. Sometimes I needed that, but often they would make assumptions about my needs, rather than just asking what I needed.

I learned to reflect on all the little things in my life that might need attending, particularly during treatment. I got more comfortable communicating those needs. This took time. I'd dimmed my voice for so long, as a new mum, wife and also as part of a big family where service to others first is an engrained part of our culture. It continues to be something I have to work on for my self-care. I slowly discovered that putting yourself first doesn't have to be selfish. It is an act and barometer of self-love which sets the standard by which the whole world will interact with you, and it enables you to sustain others.

Once people had a real sense of *what I needed* or *what I might need*, and *how* they could help, things became clearer. And it became easier to reach out.

What do you need right now?

So the question then is, what do you need? *Right now, in this moment what do you need? And what might you need in coming days, weeks and months?*

The answer didn't come easily to me at the best of times. As an Asian woman with a big family, and a toddler to care for, my needs were not something I was accustomed to thinking about.

I found it even harder during the cancer treatment, as my needs could change from day to day or even hour to hour, depending on my sleep, energy, nausea, pain and mental resilience levels.

I learnt to take moments to tune inwards and ask myself, "What do *I* need, right now, in this moment?" I got into the habit of pausing several times a day to ask this. It helped me tap into my core and nurture my soul. I continue to spend some time in silence at moments throughout the day – even if just a minute or two.

What do you need right now? In this moment? Knowing that in the next breath your needs may change.

What might you need in coming weeks and months?

Here are some ideas to get you started:

- Someone to drive you and travel with you to medical appointments.

- Someone who can help keep you company at appointments.

- Someone to support your partner or spouse.

- Someone to help with childcare, play dates, schools runs and generally be present with your kids.

- Someone who can offer recommendations for books, music, films, tv shows (I sought light, uplifting ones that needed little concentration).

- Someone who can provide recommendations for complementary therapists to help with nutritional needs, energy levels, insomnia, relaxation e.g. an acupuncturist, masseuse or reflexologist (your specialist nurse or support group may be able to advise on this).

- Someone to come sit quietly with you, hold your hand and lend a listening ear.

- Someone qualified to give you finance advice (again your hospital or local support group may be able to help).

- Someone to offer spiritual and religious guidance.

- Someone who's willing to be a walking buddy to help you sip some fresh air now and then.

Accepting help – get used to saying "yes"

When people offer help, get used to saying yes. Even if you haven't quite worked out what you need yet. You may not need the help immediately, but you may later. If you say no and insist that you are fine, people will take you at your word. Eventually they may stop asking.

I learnt that there is grace and healing in letting people in. Again, it takes courage and vulnerability. You will instinctively know the people you feel comfortable helping you. For the giver, it is often a mere small act of kindness. But for the receiver it is an intensely humbling experience and can mean the world in times of crisis. Plus, many small acts of kindness can add up to something pretty big and special. It can be life-affirming for both the recipient and the giver, who might otherwise feel helpless.

It took time for me to get used to saying "yes" – more in hope than in expectation since I knew people are busy and their ability to help could change. Some phrases I used were: *Thank you, that would be wonderful. Please can you coordinate with X?/ We're covered for now but I may need your help later./ Thank you, I'm ok for now. Is it ok if I write down your kind offer and keep it in my back pocket in case I need you later?/I have a little box with notes of offers from friends – may I add your kind offer in case I need it later?*

> *How are you with accepting help?*
> *Does it come easily?*
> *How might you get more comfortable with saying "yes"?*

Your Tree

In my past life before my cancer, I often took a lot on my own shoulders. It took time to learn to be vulnerable and ask for help. Then, I found my Tree. Family, friends and even strangers who helped ease the burden.

If you were to describe your own Tree of life what would it look like?
Cancer can touch every aspect of your life – who may be able to support you?
Sketch on the next page or maybe ask a loved one to help you. Add branches, roots and leaves to this tree. Add everyone you can think of who may be able to support you over the coming weeks and months. Your family, close friends, colleagues, medical team, neighbours, delivery drivers, charities, an accredited complementary therapist.
Keep adding to your tree. Who are your roots, trunk, leaves and branches?

Asking for help

Once I got used to working out my needs and accepting help, it also became a little easier to *ask* for help.

It certainly didn't come naturally to me. It remains something I still have to remind myself of in times of extreme stress. As a child, my mum used to trace the wide gap between my life and head lines on my birth hand, sighing with playful exaggeration at how the lines foretell how independent I am. Raised amid hidden artists and artisans, I was taught to be self-sufficient and capable of supporting others around me, both through my education and creative pursuits. Whether through earning a good living, cooking a hearty meal for large numbers of unexpected visitors, attending to a garden or a child, or knowing my way around a toolbox for essential household DIY. Add to that my family's reluctance to "trouble" others and ask for help, despite their own strong sense of *seva* to support those in distress.

So I had to learn to retrain myself. I learned a couple of stock phrases: *"I'm OK right now, I promise I'll ask if I need help, so long as you promise to tell me if it becomes a problem"*. And then, I did. Sometimes, I'd simply ask people to pray for me or send me positive vibes. Or I'd ask for recommendations for any uplifting and light books, audiobooks, music, series or films. This led to a hand-curated list of joys from my favourite people that I could dip into, depending on my mood and energy levels. It made me feel as if they were right there beside me.

I never hit rock bottom —
You never let me.
You crossed arms with strangers,
Held tight and caught me
Until I could fly again
Until my body remembered itself
and my spirit could soar once more
You flung me back up
to reach for the stars
reminding me who I was
Over and over again
Never letting me hit rock bottom
#Family

Preparing for medical appointments

Medical appointments can be a scary and lonely process. As a lawyer I was used to advocating for others. Less so for myself, particularly when I was at my lowest. I soon learnt I wasn't alone. I had a nurse specialist who would guide me through things the doctors would say and who was aware of my wider home situation. There were also small things I could do to help myself prepare for the appointments that helped steady the nerves and lead to more satisfactory discussions with my medical team.

The old adage, "look good, feel better" often helped, even when I really felt terrible - a favourite item of clothing or jewellery could boost my confidence. Listening to uplifting music always helped soothe my spirit. A treat at a local café or meeting a friend if I had the energy were things to look forward to after appointments.

In yogic tradition sitting straight and keeping your chin slightly raised can help you be more receptive and bring the body a little ease. So, remembering my dad's frequent reminder, "Chin up, Rash," literally made me sit taller and listen more attentively. Keeping my notebook nearby meant I didn't need to keep everything in my head, including my top 3 questions to ask the doctors. If I could manage nothing else, just before any appointment, a few deep breaths and focussing on extending the exhale slightly soothed my nerves and mind.

For me, the real gamechanger was finding a little head and heartspace through a moment of silent prayer or meditation before the appointment. It enabled me to visualise the outcome I sought, to give thanks to my medics and the wider hospital team around them, all focussing on my recovery. A couple of times these moments of silence would invoke golden bubbles of honeycomb light surrounding me and bursting with healing energy. Or trees reminding me to stand tall, raise my crown to the sky, root my feet to the Earth, and to breathe. Grounding me for whatever came next.

What makes you feel prepared and confident?
What brings you ease?
Who soothes you?
What might steady you before an appointment?
How can you be a little more tender to yourself today?

Self-care

Now is the time not just for self-care, but *extraordinary* self-care.

For me, self-care in tough times is often about the basics: nutritious food, sleep, rest and breath work. Time in nature, time in water, time with my son listening to music and moments in meditation all soothe me. Sometimes just little tweaks are needed to recalibrate and get back on track. Remembering to sit straight so my breath can flow well, taking a short power nap if night sleeps prove elusive, nourishing my body with quick and simple home-cooked food, short walks, and resting before I need to.

In ancient Indian traditions, everything we feed ourselves becomes us. Our words, those around us, the food on our plates, the environment in which we eat, the colours we wear, the posture we hold – all of it is connected. Slowing down to notice the many small things that soothe me helped. A cup of fresh mint tea, short siestas in front of a window bathing in sunbeams, tending to a houseplant, listening to a beautiful song gifted by a friend, being read to, a little massage, hearing my godmother's voice on the phone, short walks among trees, it all helped.

Before this storm, how did you keep your balance? What nourished you?

What is your self-care routine? What three things do you need each day to keep you whole?

What and who soothes you?

How is the quality of your food, sleep, rest and breath?

Without burdening or denying yourself in these tough days, are there small tweaks you can make that might let in more ease?

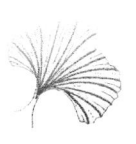

Grounding – a moment to catch your breath

When things felt a little overwhelming, I kept a few grounding techniques in my back pocket. The more I used them the more natural they became. I would use whichever one felt right for the situation. Some are rooted in my yoga practice and Indian heritage. Others are gifts from loved ones around the world.

I discovered my breath as my friend. The medical process can involve a lot of waiting. My energy levels didn't always permit me to read. I couldn't always listen to music in waiting rooms in case I missed my name being called out. So, I used any "waiting" time as a prompt to take a deep breath and follow it. Whether it was waiting for the train to take me to hospital, waiting for a noisy machine to complete a scan, or waiting anxiously for a doctor to give me my latest scan results, I trained myself to focus on my breath. When I was stripped bare and had nothing else with me – no taliswoman, no trinkets, prayer beads, "keep-safes" from loved ones, books, earphones, not even a *kara* that I've worn since birth – I could always call on my breath. I could be grateful for each one that came and passed. It became a companion and best friend for whenever I noticed I was anxious or nervous. Even two or three deep intentional breaths would stabilise me. Gently calming me, quietly disappearing, reappearing whenever I remembered it again. Always with me. It would transport me to places. To shores with waves lapping at my feet, up to the universe, down to the Earth, into my body and out of my anxiety-riddled mind.

Focussing on my breath helped lower my stress levels and calm my nervous system. It didn't stop the troublesome thoughts popping up. But I learnt to notice them, and gently bring my attention back to my breath as an anchor. If I got distracted again, it was ok. I would just guide myself back to my breath.

Taliswoman

I keep a conker in my coat pocket. I found it among fallen autumn leaves when pregnant with my son. It reminded me of the infinite potential of the life growing within me, and in us all. It is perfect in its imperfection with some knocks and scrapes along its curves. It comforts me to know it's there hidden in the folds of my coat. To rub its grooves and to marvel at the fingerprints of multiple shades of browns and reds that wave across it. Enclosing it in my palm, it would give me a second or two of familiarity and grounding before an appointment. *What keeps you grounded and protected? What helps you catch your breath? A photo, a ring, prayer beads, a sound, a scent?*

Wahe-guru

In Sikhism, 'Waheguru' means 'the (wondrous) teacher' or God. This single word is whispered into the ears of newborns and sleeping children reminding them that it is the only prayer they will ever need. I remember my great grandmother entrusting me with the word when I was a child, as if it were precious amrit (holy water) with not a drop to be spilled. It comes to my lips whenever I need it most. I would repeat 'Waheguru' slowly, bringing full attention to my in-breath and out-breath. 'Wahe' on the inhale and 'Guru' on the exhale.

Whether you believe in God or not, is there a word that has resonance and meaning for you that can help pull you back to your breath?

Five elements

In Ayurveda, everything is made of five elements: earth, fire, wind, water and ether (space). When I need a moment to ground myself I try to notice these five elements around me. For example, when having a cup of lemon and ginger tea, I visualise the hot sun (fire) that allowed the lemon and ginger to grow from the soil (earth); the warm steam that brings the aromas to my nose (air, ether); how the tea quenches my thirst (water). Doing this grounds me in the moment but also reminds me that everything is part of a whole, including myself.

White bubble

I have empathetic traits that make me sensitive to my surroundings. To protect my energy, my mum encouraged me to pause for a moment or two with a white bubble. With every in- and out-breath, I visualise a white bubble of light emanating from the centre of my forehead, expanding with each breath until it eventually surrounds me. I find it healing and comforting to bathe in this white light, even if only for a couple of moments waiting for the kettle to boil.

Balloon breath

I use a variation of this with my son, which we call 'balloon breath'. If he's anxious, I encourage him to gently extend his exhale for a count of five and allow his inhale to follow naturally, as if blowing up a big colourful balloon. He repeats it until his balloon is full.

> *What do you notice if you take a deep belly breath through your nose, and blow out through your mouth? And another. Can you manage three balloon breaths?*
>
> *How many slow exhales do you need to fill up your balloon? What colour is it? How do you feel after blowing your balloon?*

Trees

I have always been awestruck by trees. My family joke that I must have been one in my former life. Whenever I see one, touch one, sit under one, they bring me back to the here and now. I find their beauty, majesty and generosity inspiring. The wisdom and resilience of life all around us, quietly nourishing and supporting an interconnected world, asking for little in return. Friends and family, knowing of my deep affinity would send pictures of beautiful trees they encountered in whichever part of the world they were in. It unleashed a desire in them to connect with me and it fed my soul. When I passed a tree I would look up to the upturned branches, the uncanny resemblance to our own lungs, forever reminding me to breathe. To just breathe.

Bindi

My mum's best friend Anju was a second mother to me. She battled her cancer through the '90s for many years beyond her doctor's expectations, unwittingly laying down a blueprint to traverse my cancer years later. She had an infectious laugh. She was inside-out beautiful to me, always striving to look her best despite her illness. As a child I once asked her why she always wore a bindi. As if imparting a secret, she replied that it was "something really special, her third eye," and that if I *really* wanted to know she would reveal it to me later. I really wanted to know but typically of a child I ran away and forgot to ask her to complete the story. I later discovered what she meant. The bindi is not just decoration. It is placed on the base of our consciousness, where we receive wisdom from our ancestors, and connect with our inner world. Even now, when I wear one, catching a glimpse of my bindi reminds me that all the strength, courage and wisdom I need is already there – within. The breathing techniques above can be done in conjunction with bringing attention to the third eye. Simply close your eyes and gently bring your loving attention to the space between your eyes on your brow bone.

Within me
My core
My Kaur
My coeur.
#WarriorLionessHeart

A gift to me
Each new day.
A reminder of my conscience, my greatness,
Of conscious action and conscious being.
The place of my grandfather's kiss and my grandmother's light,
That even though we are apart I am not alone as
You all flow in me,
Twinkling ancestors through my veins.
Reminding me that all the strength and courage I need is right here,
Within me.
And that even when I forget, it's ok.
I just have to take a breath, go gently and
Start again.
#EverydayBindi #Anju

Rest before you need to

"Rest before you need to" was the advice from my dear friend Claire in Brussels. "*Sometimes when you feel overwhelmed and you don't know what else to do, Rashmin, just sit or lie down for a moment. Wherever you are. And rest.*"

In today's world, overworking is glamourised and busyness has become normal business. Slowly we are discovering the need to deglamourise the disease of burn-out culture given the *dis*-ease it creates. We seem to have lost focus. We have forgotten not only the importance of rest, but *how* to rest. We go robotically from one thing to the next with little time to pause or observe how we got there.

But with rest comes healing, rejuvenation and even wisdom. For our bodies, minds and soul. It still doesn't always flow naturally to me, and as a busy working single parent it can be hard to step back and know that rest will serve me (and those around me). So I've trained myself to take microbreaks throughout the day, listen to my body and plan so my week is not overscheduled. For me, a 15-minute power nap, my morning meditation, yoga and writing practice, listening to music, or lying on the grass and cloud watching does wonders.

When did you last rest?
What brings you rest?
How will you rest today?

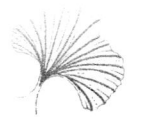

I found this in a magazine once and kept it as a reminder:

Pause
For 10 seconds to take a deep breath
For 1 minute to take in the view
For a couple of minutes to brew a cuppa
For 10 minutes to clear your head
For 20 minutes to call your mum
For half an hour to exercise your body
For a couple of hours to read a good book
For a day to find some fun,
For a weekend under the stars,
For a fortnight to recharge your batteries,
For a month to learn something new,
For a summer to be a kid again,
For a year to see the world,
For a lifetime to work out what it all means
Or for just five minutes to do absolutely nothing

Anonymous

Gratitude

Everything I am is down to my parents. They are among the most compassionate, generous, resourceful and flexible people I know. Their resilience amid life's challenges showed me how to overcome my own periods of adversity. Through some kind of osmosis, it remains the most important gift they passed to me and my brother. When we were children, they gave us enough insight into the harsh realities of the world without making it our burden. With every rising sun and moon they taught us to count each blessing, no matter what else was happening in our lives. To trust that life had a tendency to work itself out. And to rest in an abundance mindset rather than one of lack.

Now as my son lays his head on his pillow each night, I ask him to offer one prayer or blessing, and one note of thanks for one thing from the day. He grumbles about it, but I think he secretly likes it. With his sleepy eyelids fluttering down, he often conjures up something small but beautiful and unexpected.

A snuggle on the couch with my mum.
Having a garden I can play in.
My family.
My playdate with my best friend.
Being selected for a rugby tournament.

In this moment, no matter how big or small, what one thing are you grateful for?

*The blessing of knowing
In each cell of my being,
That for every day and night,
For forty years,
A prayer has been whispered
Up to ancestral stars and beyond,
For peace in my heart and
wellness in my body,
By those whose blood
Flows through mine.*
#RaisedByQueens

Joy – ramping up the positives

Ramping up the positives and mini everyday joys in my life helped me soften the bumps of the darker and lonelier days of my cancer. It was a simple idea that any of the bad things that were happening might be neutralised by something good. The good things didn't have to be big. They were often small given my low energy levels. I tried to embrace the slower pace which allowed me to notice the positives around me more. I'd allow all my senses to take in a long shower or a soak in the bath surrounded by candlelight. I'd relish a slow cup of tea in the garden. I'd treasure snuggling with my son at bedtime as he watched my finger trace the words in his book as he sounded them out. I'd take moments to examine the grooves of the hieroglyphic eye shapes on the trunk of the walnut tree in my garden, standing tall like a totem pole. I'd find time to discover new radio stations and truly listen to a piece of music I'd heard a thousand times before, but not really understood.

On walks back home from the childminder I'd play a game with my son. He had to name all the sounds he could hear. This made me think of my favourite sounds: my son's giggling when I tickle him; bamboo rustling in a breeze; falling asleep to rain pattering on the window; waves against the shore; the crunch of dry leaves underfoot on an autumn walk; the tinkle of the two golden bangles on my mum's wrist as she tidied the house or massaged us as kids; my great grandmother whispering a prayer into my ear.

Immersing myself in art or nature made me feel both small and connected with my world. Sometimes, after a medical appointment, I had the energy to spend some time at a museum exhibit near the hospital. Other times I'd have just enough for a cup of tea in a café and gaze out to the park, or rest wearily on the entrance wall to the church on Onslow Square. Each time, I left with my heart feeling replete because I had touched something bigger than myself and my current concerns. I was part of a whole.

Importantly, on the days I struggled to see the positives and joy, I tried to remember that tomorrow might feel different.

> *How can you ramp up your simple everyday positives?*
> *What little thing will you do today that's special?*
> *Where do you want to invest your love and energy?*
> *What are your favourite sounds? What sounds can you hear right now?*

The hazy slit between worlds
The sound of blood rushing to my ears and my soft heartbeat
The padded pitter patter of little feet and
A whoosh-landing on top of me.
#MorningMama!" #Arun

Odd as it may sound, if this period in your life were in fact a gift, a chance to slow down, what precious things might you notice around you?

Where do you go to feel joy or part of something bigger than yourself?

Every now and then
A deep-seated need pulses within me
To go somewhere bigger than me
To remind me how small I am
To immerse myself in an ocean
To be towered by ancient trees
To claw my fingernails deep in Earth.
Every now and then
That familiar call to
A temple to art
A temple to trees
A temple to origin
A temple to faith
A temple to silence
And find there, myself.
#SomewhereBigger

The whole Earth is a consecrated space.

We just forgot to remove our shoes and bow our heads.

#Waherguruji'sBlessing

Children

Kids sense everything, even the tiniest of them. During my cancer treatment I knew my son was feeling the transitions and my absence. Whether because I was at (or recovering from) medical appointments, or because of changes to his routine as my mum and godmother helped care for him to care for me during this period. A low point was when I returned home after my surgery, desperate to see him. He ran away from me and hid behind my mum. He refused to talk to me, perhaps articulating his anger and own loss and confusion that I'd abandoned him. It was heartbreaking.

It took time to regain his trust. We had to perfect a new cuddle to avoid my stitches bursting. He would slowly reverse into my arms and receive my hug. I borrowed a phrase from my Spanish friend, Jaime, who'd lost his own mother to cancer. I'd ask my son, *"What shall we do today that's special?"* He got to choose. Usually, he would only need 10 or 15 minutes of loving focused attention. But it made his day and meant he had some of my time every day. It might be doing a puzzle together, a family drawing competition (where we all had to draw an item, and to his delight, he also got to judge the winner), me reading a book to him, or him pretending to "read" his favourite rote-learned book to me about a famous talking train. Or just sitting on the sofa together quietly watching his favourite programme. It was and remains *our* time. Even today when life's busyness takes over I have to remind myself to safeguard this time for us.

What little thing will you do today that's special to you?

So as I tuck you in each night
And you cling on like a koala
Lying as close as you possibly could
Your big sleepy lids fluttering down
And soft soles warm against my thighs
Grumbling "Do we have to go to bed, Mama?" just as
I did many moons ago
We give thanks for the food in our tummies, the roof over our heads,
The hearts beating in our chests,
That our friends and family are safe, protected and well.
As we count each blessing of the day
Realising each one shines against the deep navy sky
I finally understand the mantra I've repeated each night
For as long as I can remember,
Its power and beauty.
So tonight, I cast this veil up to the stars
To protect us all.

#KirpaKaro #Nightblessings

Hope

Cancer taught me about hope. When I was at my lowest and there seemed to be little else, there was hope. It also brought many of life's unexplained mysteries and synchronicities.

At the same time as I was having treatment a friend's father was undergoing cancer treatment in my hospital. And then in a strange twist of fate, one of the dearest people in my life, an uncle (by love rather than blood) also began prostate cancer treatment in the same hospital as me, and to a similar schedule. He had loved and cared for his own beautiful wife – my mum's best friend Anju – when she had been diagnosed with breast cancer. She had eventually lost her long battle but not before confounding countless doctors' predictions. Unwittingly she'd enabled me to absorb her strength and dignity, tips and determination, simply by letting me observe her journey. Going through our respective treatments, my uncle and I, it was hard to coordinate spending time together at this time. It turned out we didn't need to. Sometimes I'd be thinking of him as I approached the hospital, then I'd turn a corner and he'd be right there. Or I'd receive a text from him, right at that moment. Or see him in my waiting room. Or on the tube. Like a guardian angel he managed to be there when I needed him most. Perhaps, also, when he needed me.

Whenever I looked into my 2-year old's eyes, all I could see was hope. Whilst I wrote this poem when learning to navigate single motherhood during the first Covid-19 lockdowns, it also reminds me of our nights curled up together during my cancer treatment.

You say I look beautiful but
Sometimes I feel so fragile
That a tiny breeze could set me off track
Then my eyes meet yours
And I catch my breath
And I remember my wings are made of silk
Soft and strong
And wherever we land
we will be just fine.

#Arun

Light

Growing up, each and every evening that I can remember, my parents used to light a little diya in a corner of our home. It brought a moment for reflection and thanks. Its flame radiated warmth and comfort far greater than its size. I have continued the same ritual for my own family.[1]

For me, some of life's most memorable experiences have centred around light. Golden honeycomb bubbles of light and oxygen gently cossetting me in meditation. A ray of sunlight bouncing off a crystal hanging on the acer in my garden and onto my forehead reminding me of my grandmother's kiss. My first "proper" writer's experience was when I rocked up to what I thought was an online lecture by the brilliant Eve Makis in my sweaty gym kit, only to find I was to participate in a poetry workshop on my name (I wrote about how my parents wished to create *beams of silky light*). Opening my eyes from

---

[1] Please be careful when tired, or around kids and pets when lighting a candle

meditation to notice shades and gradations of shadows created by light, as if wearing new glasses. Fields of sunflowers evoking a walk with my friend Julia's uncle reminding us, "Richtung Sonne", follow the direction of the sun. Stumbling across the startling beautiful, accurate and yet untranslatable Japanese word *komorebi;* discussions with my friend Claire (whose name also means *light*) concluding with the translation *the light and shadow dance created by sunlight filtering through trees.* Another friend, Leila, introducing me to the Japanese art of *kintsukuroi* where broken porcelain vessels are repaired by pouring gold into the cracks. The very site of the breakage becomes the most valuable and beautiful part. Perhaps representing how golden light can shine even through our most broken pieces, if we let it.

> *What does light mean to you? When do you notice it changing most?*
> *What type of light soothes you?*
> *When did you last bathe in sun or moonlight?*
> *What if your scars are, in fact, the most beautiful parts of you? The parts where light shines through.*

Energy

On my toughest days, when my energy and mood were low, I could catch myself veering into self-pity. I knew I had to shift the energy. What worked for me? Simple things. Opening a window to get some fresh oxygen flowing, lighting a candle, and often, just moving helped change perspective – into the garden, around the block or up the stairs, dancing in the kitchen with my son, or simply stretching in my chair. Some days nothing seemed to work, but at least I had tried.

What helps you shift your energy on your tough days?
What song do you love dancing to? What was the song you loved to dance to as a child? When did you last dance to it?
What can you shed which no longer serves you today? How can you make way for new energy?

"Feeling the feels" and a note on positivity

My Indian family and community include some of the most positive people I know. Rooted in faith, positive outlooks and the ability to accept whatever life throws our way, appreciation that some things will always remain a mystery, and that against the odds life will somehow work itself out all runs in our DNA.

I am also naturally predisposed and conditioned to seek the silver lining. However, at times in my cancer journey the pressure to be positive sometimes made me feel unseen, unheard and even forced me to mask my true emotions. There were many times that I felt anything but positive. That's not to say I had given up on life – I was determined to survive, from the outset. Yet there were times when I wrestled with the uncertainty of whether I'd see my son grow up, what treatment lay ahead, fear of loss of pieces of me, and pain management. Rainy days did come. I could oscillate between being scared, anxious, angry, frustrated, blue, to feeling happy all within the course of a day or even an hour.

At one point, I recall asking family to stay positive around me. I couldn't carry their grief as well as my own. I soon realised this only covered up my true feelings and theirs. I discovered the only answer was to be truthful with myself, to really "feel the feels" as someone once put it to me. To recognise them, sit with them, and let them pass like weather. Knowing the next moment could be sunny, or stormy. But that that too, would pass. Being honest with myself meant I could be more honest with others. It didn't mean I had to tell everyone how I felt all the time, as that would be exhausting at a time when I needed to conserve my energy and life force, but telling one or two trusted people provided balm for my soul. It takes courage to do so.

When do you allow yourself to feel?
How do you tend to do this?
Talking to someone?
Keeping a diary?
Sitting in silence?
Singing? Listening to music?
Something else?

Bravery

Upon hearing of my diagnosis, my dad's sister, Booji, who I grew up with, an exceptional gardener, cook and creative said to me, *"You're going to have to be braver than you've ever been before."*

The words stuck and forced me to think about the bravest people I've known in life. It evoked my ancestors who made decisions to uproot and re-root their families in search of a better life, embedding grit and determination into our blood along the way. Somehow the knowledge of their strength held me up.

Years later, when my son was seven, he completed some homework on what bravery means to him. He wrote, "it means carrying your courage." I loved this gentle and beautiful observation. The Latin root of the word "courage" is "cor", which means the heart. Even when you're exhausted, even when your courage wants to run away and hide, perhaps being brave means gently carrying it.

What does bravery mean to you?
When did you last feel brave?
Who or what makes you brave?

When I feel lonely,
I still myself and
remember all it took
to get me here.

I cast my heart heavenwards and
back down to all those
who eased my path

Invoking the spirit of my ancestors
known and unknown
sparkling in my blood

I marvel at the millions of years of their
sliding doors, chance meetings
trials and error, lucky escapes and
stories of survival
that led to my being

As if the whole universe
and all of time
conspired for me to be
right here
in this moment

Just to tell me
I am not and
never have been
Alone.

Creativity

I once confided in my neighbour Julia that I was struggling to cope with the manifold emotions that my diagnosis had brought up. She reflected that it might help if I were able to find a creative outlet to engross me and help me work through things.

That's how I rediscovered gardening and writing. Immersing my hands in soil and patiently working with the small patch of earth around me opened my heart to tears that would spill into my journal. Those words slowly formed the beginnings of poems, including some in this book.

I still find it helps me to take a few minutes each evening with a cup of tea to reflect on the day that has been and visualise the day ahead. It has allowed me to let go off the day and be ok with whatever I couldn't accomplish, remembering that tomorrow is a new day.

Everyone is born creative. Even when I'm short on time, writing, cooking, being in nature, playing with textiles and colours in my dress, playing with my son, dancing in the kitchen, and surrounding my home with colour, music and art keep my creative well topped up.

How do you like to fill your creative well?
How do you express yourself?
How can you amplify the creativity in your life, even just a little?
What makes your heart sing and your soul soar?
What's going on that you can channel into a creation?

Stillness and silence

Oftentimes, the solace and answers I need are found in silence and stillness. Maybe one day I will discover that prayers, blessings, yoga and meditation are all one. For now, my sense is that prayers and blessings are something external, between me and a higher energy, while yoga and meditation are internal; a tapping into my inner self, but which connects me with my outer world. I need both and I need stillness and silence to access both.

Throughout my cancer, sitting with whatever came up in stillness, without judgment, was hard but necessary. I tried to welcome each visiting thought and emotion as a friend, and then let them go along their way. Each was a teacher helping me tune in to how I was in that moment. At times, it could be so overwhelming I'd intentionally avoid yoga and meditation for days, as I wasn't ready for the lesson. I didn't feel strong enough to greet the visitors. Gradually I learnt that even a couple of minutes could help me accept their presence and ease my racing mind and worried heart. Not doing so meant all the visitors ended up waiting in agitation outside my front door, only to burst open the door and overwhelm me.

One night in hospital after surgery I was in intense pain in my whole body. Visiting hours were long over, my mum had blown me a goodnight kiss, patients were sleeping and overworked nurses were dealing with other patients. In my pain-induced sleepless state, I felt the clear presence of Guru Gobind Singh Ji, the 10th Sikh Guru, turning from the portrait on my bedside and blowing me a kiss of healing white light straight to the wound in my chest. I somehow knew my mum was sending prayers of healing light to me from home.

I welcomed our Guru's cool breath to the source of the pain. It showed me that the pain was in fact emanating from a small 10x10 cm area, but my mind had amplified it and tensed up my entire body so that every organ felt it was under attack. Whilst I waited for the busy night nurses' assistance, I recalled the lessons from my yoga teachers for pain management: slightly extend and focus on the out-breath and the in-breath will follow naturally. Slowly and surely, the body relaxed, my mind gently easing with it. The pain was still there but much more manageable. The whole experience still gives me goosebumps. It taught me how interwoven mind, body and soul are. And that alongside the medical care, I had some power to amplify or reduce my own suffering.

But what if you can't bring yourself to pray, or to call on the energy of the universe? Or even know what to ask for? I often found myself this way, lost as to what to ask for, or how to ask for it. In those moments, I learnt to still myself. To sit still for a few deep breaths, focussing on my out-breath. Or to lie down and let the Earth support me as I closed my eyes and drew my attention to the rise and fall of each breath. A few minutes of stillness peppered through the day.

> *How do you still yourself?*
> *Are there meditations that work for you?*
> *What comes up for you in stillness?*
> *How might you include 10 minutes of silence and stillness into your day? What do you notice?*

Prayer

People often asked me how they could help me. When I didn't know, I would simply ask them to convert their worries into prayers or good wishes. I could feel that protective energy flowing in from the world over.

But it was only relatively recently that I learnt to pray - for myself. Somewhere along the way as a child, I mistakenly thought that *seva (selfless service for one's world, a tenet of Sikhism)* meant you should pray for others above yourself as their needs are greater than your own. It took me time to learn that whilst this is important, it is also ok to pray for yourself, that I too am worthy of this. Praying for oneself is not egotistical or selfish. It is an act of self-compassion and helps manifest your dreams.

There remained days when I was so lost I didn't know where to start with my own prayers; I was too weak, scared to be vulnerable, and afraid of what I might invoke as it made it all too real. For those times, beautiful people prayed for me anyway. When I lost my voice and couldn't find the words, they used theirs. When I couldn't even muster a silent prayer, they sang out boldly, for the whole universe to hear. Marlene who helped clean my home asked her prayer circle at her Polish church to pray for my protection, my mum's friends would text me prayers they'd curated for me. Strangers I'd never met, palms pressed, encircled me with their love, energy, spirit, intention, language and hearts. All I had to do was receive it. Even if my relationship with God was at times uneasy and evolving.

Another Claire in my life who reintroduced me to writing once sent me a message, "I'm going to pray for you. Tell me, is there something specific you'd like me to pray for?" It was such a humbling gift and one I'd never received before. I always felt so blessed to feel the prayers of my parents, grandparents and godmother every day and night that I've lived. But to be asked by someone what they should specifically channel their energy and prayers into felt empowering. It required me to take a breath and work out what *I* most needed in that moment, in itself an act of vulnerability. This, in turn, helped me re-find my voice to lift my own prayers for others, and myself.

When in need, is there a prayer that comes to your lips, or an image that comes to your heart?
Do you remember one from your childhood?

Or, if you were to summon the life force of the universe right now, what would you ask for?
In this moment, on this day, what would you like someone to wish for you, or pray for you? Be as specific as you can.

For friends and family

When cancer hits, much attention is given to the person who has received the cancer diagnosis. Yet the potential impacts can go far wider. Feeling helpless, many people have asked me how they might support loved ones going through cancer. This is usually what I invite them to consider.

Consider grounding yourself first and processing your own emotions before meeting your loved ones, so you can be present and really listen, and not accidentally impose your own grief on top of theirs.

Patiently accept that it is for your loved one to decide what they wish to share, with whom and when. It can be exhausting retelling the same story at a time when the person needs to conserve their energy. In time, they may need your help with this.

On hearing the news of a cancer diagnosis there can be a sudden impulse to reach out and "do something" to help. Immediate outpourings of love can be life-affirming, but also overwhelming. So consider with sensitivity when the best time to reach out might be and what message you wish to share.

Appreciate that each cancer is different. Each person is different. Their needs are different - and can change. So, ask what help may be needed.

Ask yourself honestly how you might be able to help, and let your loved one know. Recognise that they may not need help immediately but they may need to draw on you later.

Being honest with yourself and them from the outset about what you can and can't commit to will help manage expectations, avoid overpromising and minimise misunderstandings. When someone is vulnerable they need reliable and trusted sources of support.

Remember that whatever you offer doesn't have to be something "big". Often the person just needs a little support. And lots of small kindnesses from many people can amount to something big. It's not all on you.

Gift ideas

Showing someone you care and that you are there need not cost a lot of time or money. Often the smallest things raised my spirits, like a drawing by a friend's child or a posy of daisies and dandelions they had picked in the garden. You will know your loved one best and what brings them joy. If you're unsure what they need right now consider asking, if the time is right.

These are ideas of gifts I really appreciated -

A list of uplifting, light and easy songs, movies, books and audiobooks from family and friends curated for me (audiobooks were particularly helpful when my eyes needed to rest). For inspiration, a collection of uplifting music I've discovered can be found at Spotify under *Falling Leaves and Flying Butterflies*.

Notes with uplifting prayers, pictures, photos and poems. In today's world technology helps us connect quickly with texts and emails. But for me personally, receiving a hand-written note or letter meant a great deal.

My friend Suzy sought to create a collective care package for one of her friends and asked for suggestions on what to include to boost their spirits. As well as small hand creams, candles, and the ideas above, I suggested a small note book for sketches, doodles, journaling or to record endless numbers of doctor's names, appointments, medications and hospital numbers.

Keeping a list of practical offers of support from family and friends can also help. This might include drivers for appointments, making a meal or stocking some healthy food in the freezer, babysitting, picking up groceries, calling for a chat, sending music or tv tips, doing chores around the house, and school runs.

If sending a brief note, text or email to a loved one with cancer, I often remind the person that "there is no need to reply, I'm just sending my love and thoughts" so they don't feel the burden of having to respond at a time when they need to conserve their energy.

Contact details of reputable local practitioners of complementary treatment at the hospital, nearby support centres, or accredited private providers, such as for acupunture, massage, manicures, talking therapies, yoga and meditation, reflexology and other treats or wellbeing remedies.

Consider whether any specific support can be offered to other family members to alleviate their burden and offer respite.

My Tree

This book started as an impulse to help someone I love who was far away. Someone who does much for her community, but who during the global pandemic was isolated in the North-West Territories of Canada, and wrestling with her own state of emergency; a cancer scare. She was aware of my cancer diagnosis years earlier and bravely reached out.

The SOS from my cousin was sandwiched between the loss of two dear friends from cancer. They never met but were kindred spirits. The pandemic brought news of more loved ones facing cancer, often without the holistic support I'd accessed when facing mine.

Working for a humanitarian aid charity at the time, I wondered if I could draw on lessons from peacetime war and disaster prevention and preparedness so we are better equipped when bad news hits. What if, in the early days of a cancer diagnosis, before the fast and furious medical process starts, we can breathe deeply, draw on our inner compass and the support around us to help steady ourselves for whatever lies ahead? What if we can gently redirect our deepest fears towards healing? Dig within ourselves to hidden capacities of love and fortitude just waiting to be mined, both ours and others'? What if we can slowly and surely build our army, our dream team, our own Tree of support? Who remind us that whatever happens next, we are loved and not alone.

I set about curating a heartful collection of wisdom that was offered to me, to pass it on. The result, I hope, is a gentle companion for those embarking on their own cancer story. It's a ghazal of gratitude for my life and to my Tree for sustaining me. Accidentally, it became a catharsis for me too and a marker of my own (messy) evolution as a human.

My story is not one of battling cancer valiantly and emerging as a superhero. It is one of learning small lessons painfully and imperfectly, but being lucky enough to come out the other side. It's about someone who still strays sometimes, but allows life to nudge her back into remembering how precious our health is, and finding ways to nourish and celebrate it.

Epilogue

As I was finalising this book, I discovered a little lump. On the lower left side of my back, towards the spine. It seemed to be telling me that I'd been carrying too much.

It took time to have it tested and removed amid NHS strikes, long waiting lists and being shunted between different hospitals. Whilst the medical results were reassuring and the lump was not cancerous, the year-long process sent me into a spin. My mind played tricks - *they said all was fine last time and look what happened...they're not listening, something's wrong... can you really trust them?...can you really trust your body anymore?... do you even trust yourself?*

I'd weathered earlier recurrence scares so I was alarmed at how quickly I could descend into a negative spiral. The path seemed similar to the year leading to my sarcoma diagnosis – difficulty accessing medical care, long waiting lists, anxiety and loneliness from not being heard, and an understanding that I would have to be my own best advocate for my wellbeing. As the lump was not cancerous my cancer hospital could not support me, yet the general hospital I was referred to did not fully understand my cancer history, nor the emotional associations.

Then, unexpectedly, I unearthed past grief I'd been carrying, for 10 years, from my son's birth story. Whilst I thought I'd "done the work", the benign lump on my back unlocked birth trauma, feelings of being dismissed and not listened to when I repeatedly sought to raise alarm bells about his health and mine. One which I had struggled to find the words for, and so remained unspoken.

I soon found the words with the help of the wonderful Corinna, a counsellor I accessed through a BUPA-Macmillan charity scheme, which my own medics mentioned out of frustration that their hospital was unable to support me.

The short(ish) origins story of my cancer was a period of extreme stress in the two years prior to my cancer, following the birth of my beautiful son. Much investment is desperately needed into rare cancer research, but I suspect that episode ignited the weakest part of my body, a small benign lump I'd had in my breast since my 20s. The guidance back then was to leave it alone and not remove it.

Our birth story was a long and complicated saga. No single cause or perpetrator was to blame and of course life is rarely that black and white. It was more a series of mishaps, happenstances, poor communication, sliding doors, lack of care, mysteries, and likely a healthcare systems failure. Cumulatively, the events led to almost losing my son in childbirth, and then again a week after birth from severe dehydration. A combination of an undiagnosed posterior tongue tie and the early hidden growth of the sarcoma in my breast meant he had struggled to breastfeed. We got through it, just, but it left my then husband and myself in the fog of some kind of collective and individual post-traumatic stress. We desperately tried to put the past behind us, to work through it with counselling and the love of our close ones. But my body, heart and soul continued to carry the shadow of shame and unreleased trauma.

And so, to my outside world, I was a professional woman, achieving my life goals of working internationally in public service as a lawyer and diplomat, happily married, well-travelled, raising a beautiful child despite the challenges of his birth, living in a beautiful part of the world and that world was our oyster.

However, on the inside, there was so much more going on. I blamed myself for what happened, for not being more vocal, for not listening to my body, for not getting more help, even though I had tried to do all of those things. I felt inadequate both as a wife, and a mother, scared to continue to breastfeed for fear of losing our son again. I was ashamed of my secret relief at needing to abandon breastfeeding to enable a biopsy to be taken when I urged doctors to test the changing lump in my breast. The biopsy inaccurately came back clear. We later learnt the needle probably missed the "crown"-shaped mass, hitting between its prongs.

The following two years were just about survival. Despite help from loved ones and counselling the newborn and toddler days passed in a blur. We were operating on empty and unable to get on top of our sleep. My son's father poured his best self into his work, which proved addictive. I tried to balance motherhood with a demanding job, returning to work when my son was 13 months. I ate without joy, more for comfort and routine.

It was my baby boy that drew my attention to my lump. I collected him one bleak evening from his childminder, arriving late, exhausted and depleted. He refused to go in his pram on the way home so I carried him whilst pushing the pram. As the cold rain lashed down, he kept bashing his little first against my breast, where I had my old lump. He was so angry, as if he couldn't believe I couldn't see what he could see. That evening as I changed for bed, I noticed the lump had changed. It seemed different, bigger than normal, and was hurting.

Oddly, the cancer diagnosis came as a huge relief. I'd known something was wrong for a long time. I had levels of exhaustion and stomach problems I'd never known, which were dismissed by doctors as IBS and being a struggling first-time mum transitioning to the return to work. Asking for help didn't come easily for me back then. The power imbalance of repeatedly being dismissed by different doctors eventually silenced me. Until my body had no choice to speak up for itself.

The whole episode was a reminder of the complex legacy of cancer. Both the profound respect for life it gave me, but also an understanding of its fragility. Even for lucky survivors, like any loss, the grief of cancer can crop up at unexpected times and in unexpected ways, and it deserves time, patience, compassion, and acceptance to let it go and to make space for something new.

So, what do I know now that I didn't know before?

Some stories can only be told after a certain time has elapsed, from a higher place of perspective, distance and consciousness. In many ways the two years that preceded my cancer was a dress rehearsal for the cancer. It provided a blueprint for navigating it.

I learnt that no-one can take responsibility for your health and wellbeing but you. You have to proactively own it, and be your own best advocate.

That for rare cancer survivors like myself it is so vital to be seen by a specialist hospital. By doctors who've seen so many cases like yours that they see you as a "normal" patient.

That it's natural to wonder why you've got cancer but it's unlikely to yield useful answers and more likely to sap precious energy that is needed for healing.

Especially in the early days, be tender with yourself.

That it is unnerving how quickly old habits can come back in times of extreme stress. And how fear can spread like wildfire and take over if you let it, robbing you of both rationality and joy.

That even if things seem bad, or really bad, it's possible to change perspective with patience, love and support.

That my energy, life force or prana is powerful, beautiful, precious, and finite, so worthy of protection. Where my attention goes, my energy flows. So, I have to gently and consciously focus that attention. Otherwise, life and all its demands will always take my best energy away from my goals and the people that matter most to me.

For me, my "best" energy is first thing in the morning. It is when I feel connected to myself and my world, when my focus is sharp and things just flow. There is something sacred about awaking in the darkness when everyone else is still asleep, as if the whole Earth is awakening just for me. The air smells so fresh and clean when I open the windows and adjust my eyes to the rising dawn. My creativity seems to flow.

That the body, mind and soul are inextricably connected. For me being active is so important as when my body is unable to move, my mind also gets stuck.

And when I stumble, I've now learnt to be kinder to myself. To forgive myself, to trust and yield to life.

That how I see and treat myself is a mirror for how others will see me. Continuing to know myself helps me express my needs and draw my boundaries in a way that I didn't before – and surprisingly, people respect them. Especially when I do so in a way that honours my needs whilst also being aware of the needs of the collectives I belong to.

That like any loss, the dealing with and healing from cancer process is not linear. Sometimes you go forwards, sometimes backwards, sometimes you feel forever stuck. Even recurrence scares can take you through the grief cycle. But most of us have lived through past forms of loss and grief so, we already have a blueprint for recovery that we can draw from.

Then, a lesson that for those of us in leadership positions, we have work to do. How can we de-glamorize the business of busyness? How do we ensure we don't lose the positive lessons from the pandemic of finding creative ways to create more wholesome, well, and thriving teams? Where mental health is taken seriously, hidden disabilities and obstacles seen and supported, genuine and holistic team culture encouraged?

In my own workplace and in my field of international law and relations we seek to find solutions to the world's biggest pains and challenges. How can we truly do this if we don't first look inwards, take serious charge of our own health and wellbeing, and heal ourselves first? How can we bring our best to the negotiating table or board room if we haven't first resolved the conflicts within ourselves? The energy and intentionality we bring to such matters is in our gift and really matters.

How can we be more conscious and supportive of the multiple and intersectional challenges some women face throughout their cancer, and still just "get on with" as that is how we have been conditioned? It takes bold and brave workplaces to actively put wellness and wellbeing at the heart of all they do, to create space where people can talk about these issues honestly and safely, and to invest in preventative care, wellbeing, healing and an understanding of that by-gone word, convalescence. It's a big question for me to continue to explore in my own wellness and healing path, and the culture I wish to co-create with my team.

So, in the end, it seems this is an imperfect guide from someone who is still figuring it all out. A work in progress by a work in progress. In the sincere hope that perhaps in the messiness, darkness, loneliness and uncertainty and aftermath of cancer, it might provide an anchor. And a little space to breathe.

With love and healing light,
Rashmin

Shed the old, Beautiful One
Shed the cocoon of your past
Let it drop among the falling leaves

Rest among them until you're ready
To rise up

For even in these stormy times
Your wings are stronger
than first appear

#FallingLeavesFlyingButterflies

Your notes

Use these last pages to make your notes, record your own thoughts and feelings and make this book yours.

A note on the cover art

I keep seeing an image of a golden tree swaying in the breeze. Perhaps a silver birch, or gingko biloba in autumn. As buds appear the golden leaves drop to the floor like tears replenishing the Earth. There is so much life and movement in this tree. It is unclear if its leaves are falling, or butterflies are emerging.

The cover art is inspired by a single ginkgo leaf drawn with gold ink on black cartridge paper. It represents light amid darkness. Strength, despite apparent fragility. The possibility of letting go of the old and heavy to allow for lightness, new growth, and perhaps even transformation.

Gingkos are ancient and sacred trees celebrated in East Asia. The species has survived since the time of the dinosaurs and are considered a living fossil. Their leaves symbolise hope, resilience, and strength.

Acknowledgments

For Anju and Tash. All those before, in-between and after.

To my Tree.

To the wonderful Dr Miah and Dr Zaidi and my medical team at the Royal Marsden Hospital, who still treat me as the team captain.

To Ash who saw the greatness in me even in my darkest days, and with beautiful Carmen and Uma helped guide me home.

To my Claires (meaning "light") in Brussels, Brighton and Nottingham who opened their arms and doors so I could find the heartspace to let the leaves fall and butterflies fly. To Sophie for her quiet wisdom and gently sitting next to me. To Navroza, Rashnik, Lou, Carina, Matty, Jules and Gosia for your tenderness.

To Layla and Emilia, two of the most inspiring young women I know – always be brave, bold, sparkle, love and be loved. Your mum glitters through you both.

To Yuko, Akram, Sayu and family who nutured the creative in me. To Gabriela and my writing tribe - meeting you was like a homecoming. To Caz, without whom I couldn't have pulled it all (nor myself) together. To Ana who inspired me to follow my he(art) and use my own drawings. To James for his irrepressible and contagious enthusiasm, and to Chris for his gentle observations and quiet confidence in me and the book.

To Nat, for her big heart and letting me share our story. To dear Jasbir Aunty and Jaspal Uncle, who always believed in me and made the book fly. To Ira, who, just when I thought I'd given this book my all, gently urged, "Can you go a little deeper? Can you bear it?"

To Bama for her fortitude. To Ashok Uncle and Ranjit Uncle who battled alongside their wives, showing what love and seva mean in practice

To my kind, funny, unique and wise Arun. Watching you grow has been the privilege of my life. Thank you for being my best cheerleader and worst critic, and for gently asking if I'd worked on *Falling Leaves and Flying Butterflies* today. Dada and I both love you so much.

To my Deepi Massi and Dickey Uncle who showed me what love is and have loved me since forever. To Baji for his prayers and vigilance, and to Booji and Bivek for their constant love, soul and artistic guidance.

To my brother Sanjeev, who's literally held me upright on more occasions than I care to remember. And my parents, Ambi and Madhveen, who "borned me", gave me strong roots, and never stopped pouring love into me. "

Useful resources and organisations

www.sarcoma.uk
Expert advice and support from the bone and soft tissue cancer charity

www.royalmarsden.org
The Royal Marsden Cancer Charity exists to support the Royal Marsden, a world-leading cancer hospital.

www.macmillan.org.uk
Macmillan Cancer Support provides reliable cancer information, plus services for people in the UK living with cancer at every stage of their cancer experience.

www.helenanahitawilson.com
Musician Helen Anahita Wilson takes sounds derived from bioelectricity in plants with medicinal and healing properties from Chelsea Physic Garden to create music to listen to during chemotherapy. It's pretty special. All proceeds go to the cancer charity, Maggie's Centres.

Find Rashmin's *Falling Leaves and Flying Butterflies* playlist at:

> www.open.spotify.com/playlist/
> 0sB2CrVxQQ86vl4wwceTQ2

About the author

Rashmin Sagoo is a British Indian writer and creative, international lawyer, and former diplomat. Her writing centres on connection, awareness, oneness, balance, nature, love, loss and healing.

She is Director of the International Law Programme at Chatham House, having previously worked in the humanitarian, governmental and international organisations sectors. Increasingly, she wonders whether it is possible to make sense of the outer world without first unpacking one's inner world.

Instagram: @rashmin.sagoo

Printed in Great Britain
by Amazon